ROMANTIC

DINNERS

Part.1

Dorothie Laman

ROMANTIC DINNERS PART-1

by DOROTHIE LAMAN

CONCLUSION...............................134

INTRODUCTION

While we all love a night out, date nights in can be special too. When was the last time you actually hosted a romantic date night dinner for your partner? Instead of pulling those less-than-appetizing leftovers out of the freezer, you can spice up both your plate and your love life without even leaving the house—and cook up your appetites for each other in the process.

.With that in mind, this book will share a 5-course inspiring romantic dinner meal to celebrate your special love whether that be on Valentine's Day, anniversary dinners, birthday dinners, engagement dinners. Or just because!

For those of us who don't have the chef's touch, it can be intimidating to plan a meal without knowing where to start. But as it turns out, making that extravagant spread isn't as hard as it seems (and it's easier with these awesome but simple recipes!).

ROMANTIC APPETIZER

1. Bacon and Smoked Oysters

- 2 can Smoked oysters
- 1/4 cup Light vegetable oil
- 1/2 lb Bacon strips
- 40 Round wooden toothpicks
- 3 tb Garlic, minced

a) Cut bacon strips in thirds.

b) Wrap a bacon slice around each oyster and place a toothpick through to hold it in place.

c) In a medium skillet, heat oil, and add garlic.

d) Cook wrapped oysters in oil until bacon is crisp.

e) Remove from pan and drain on a paper towel to drain.

2. Blue Cheese and Walnuts Appetizers

- 1 cup Walnuts

- 1-cup Crumbled blue cheese

- 1 Egg beaten with 1 tab water

a) Just chop 1 cup of walnuts (depending on the size of brie you need to cover) and stir into 1 cup crumbled blue cheese. Press onto the top of the Brie and carefully wrap a sheet of thawed puff pastry dough (Roll out to size needed).

b) Use fingers wet with cold water to seal underside of pastry. Cut off excess to make cutouts and adhere to top of Brie with a little cold water.

c) Brush with egg mixture.

d) Bake on a cookie sheet covered with baking parchment in a 375-degree oven for about 20 minutes until golden. (Parchment makes it simple to transfer Brie to serving dish.) Let Baked Brie stand for 20-30 Min. before cutting to let it firm up a little.

3. Buffalo Wings with Cheese Sauce

- 6 tb Butter or margarine

- 1/4 c Hot pepper sauce

- Vegetable oil for frying

- 18 Chicken wings, disjointed, tips discarded
Blue Cheese Dipping Sauce:

- 1/4 lb Blue cheese, Roquefort or Gorgonzola

- 1/2 c Mayonnaise

- 1/2 c Sour cream

- 1 tb Lemon juice

- 1 tb Wine vinegar

- Hot pepper sauce to taste

a) Melt butter in a small saucepan. Add hot sauce and remove from the heat.

b) In a large frying pan or deep-fat fryer, heat 1" of oil to 375. Fry wings in batches without crowding until golden brown, 12 1/2 minutes. Drain on paper towels.

c) Brush wings with spicy butter. Serve warm with Blue Cheese Dipping Sauce.

d) For Blue Cheese Dipping Sauce:

e)

f) In small bowl, mash the blue cheese, leaving some small lumps. Whisk in the mayonnaise until blended. Add the sour cream, lemon juice,

g) wine vinegar, and hot pepper sauce; whisk until well blended.

h) Cover and refrigerate until ready to serve

4. Caviar Heart Kisses

- 1 sm Cucumber, scrubbed and trimmed

- 1/3 c Sour Cream

- 1 ts Dried dill weed

- Freshly ground black pepper to taste

- 1   Jar red salmon caviar

- Fresh dill sprigs

- 8   Thin slices whole-wheat bread

- Butter or margarine

a) Slice cucumber into 1/4-inch rounds.

b) In a small bowl, combine sour cream, dried dill and pepper. Place one teaspoon of the sour cream mixture on each cucumber slice. Garnish each with about 1/2-teaspoon caviar and a dill sprig.

c) Cut bread slices with heart-shaped cookie cutter. Toast and butter. Place cucumber slices in centre of serving plate and surround with toast hearts.

5. Cheddar and Broccoli Appetizers

10 oz Frozen chopped broccoli*

- 8 oz Whole kernel corn; drained
- 1/4 c Onion; chopped
- 1/2 c Walnuts; coarsely chopped
- 1/2 c Milk
- 1/4 c Butter; melted
- 2 Eggs
- 1/2 c Bisquick
- 1/4 ts Garlic salt

- 1 c Cheddar cheese; shredded

a) Heat oven to 375. Grease a 9x9x2" pan.

b) Mix broccoli, corn, onion and walnuts. Place in pan.

c) Beat milk, butter, eggs, bisquick and garlic salt until smooth, 15 seconds. in blender on high, stopping blender frequently to scrape sides if necessary, or 1 minute. with electric mixer on high. Pour evenly into pan.

d) Bake until knife inserted in centre comes out clean, 23-25 minutes.; sprinkle with cheese.

e) Bake until cheese is melted, 2-3 minutes longer. cool 30 minutes. Cut into triangles or squares. Makes 30 appetizers.

6. Cheese and Sausage Snacks

- 1 Roll Sausage Meat

- 1 Spanish Onion, finely chopped

- 1 lb Grated Cheddar Cheese

- 3 c Bisquick

- 3/4 c Milk

a) Blend sausage meat and onion in blender. Add the cheddar, bisquick, and milk and mix well.

b) Drop from teaspoon onto greased cookie sheet Bake at 425 Degrees Fahreneheit for 10 -15 minutes or until browned.

7. Clam Stuffed Mushroom Caps

- 1/2 c Butter
- 2 lb Mushrooms, 1-1/2" to 2" in diameter
- 1 c Minced clams, with liquid
- 1 Clove garlic, minced
- 1/2 c Dried bread crumbs
- 1/3 c Parsley, chopped
- 3/4 ts Salt

- 1/4 ts Ground black pepper

- Lemon juice

a) Melt butter in sauce pan.

b) Remove and dice mushrooms stems. Dip mushroom caps in butter and place, rounded side down, on a rack on a cookie sheet.

c) Drain clams and reserve liquid.

d) In melted butter, saute mushrooms stems and garlic. Add clam liquid and simmer until mushroom stems are tender. Remove from heat and stir in the bread crumbs, parsley, salt and pepper.

e) Spoon mixture into mushroom caps. Broil about 6 " from heat for about 8 minutes, until mushrooms are tender and tops are lightly browned. Sprinkle a few drops of lemon juice on each and serve hot.

ROMANTIC DINNERS

8. Chicken in Silky Almond Sauce

- 16 ea pieces skinned chicken

- 5 ea medium onions thin sliced

- 2 tb vegetable oil

- 6 tb blanched ground almonds

- 3 tb ground coriander

- 2 tb chopped fresh ginger
- 2 ts ground cardamom
- 1 x course salt
- 2 ts ground red pepper
- 1 ts ground cumin
- 1/2 ts ground fennel
- 1/2 c vegetable oil
- 2 c plain yogurt
- 1 c water
- 1 x fresh cilantro (garnish)

a) Pat chicken dry.

b) Heat 2 tablespoons of vegetable oil in a heavy large skillet over medium-high heat.

c) Add chicken in batches and cook on all sides just until no longer pink (do not brown).

d) Remove using slotted spoon and set aside.

e) Heat 1/2 cup vegetable oil in skillet. Add sliced onion and fry until wilted and pale brown, stirring constantly, about 10 minutes.

f) Stir in almonds, coriander, ginger, cardamom, salt, ground red pepper, cumin and fennel and cook 3 to 5 more minutes. Remove mixture from heat.

g) Transfer half of the mixture to processor or blender. Puree with 1/2 of the yogurt and 1/2 of the water.

h) Repeat with the rest of the mixture, yogurt and water.

i) Pour sauce back into skillet.

j) Add chicken to skillet. Place over medium-high heat and bring to a boil.

k) Reduce heat, cover and simmer until chicken is tender and sauce is thickened, about 45 minutes.

l) Remove from heat. Let stand at room temperature for about 30 minutes.

m) Transfer to serving dish, garnish with cilantro and serve immediately.

9. Steak with tarragon mushrooms

INGREDIENTS

STEAKS

- 1 teaspoon canola oil

- 2 1 ½ inch-thick filet mignon steaks, aka big sexy steaks, 12 to 14 ounces total

- ½ teaspoons each kosher salt and freshly ground pepper

- 1 large shallot, minced

- ½ teaspoon chopped fresh thyme

- 1/4 cup sweet vermouth

- 3/4 cup reduced-sodium chicken or beef broth

- $\frac{1}{2}$ teaspoon corn starch or arrowroot

TARRAGON MUSHROOMS

- 2 teaspoons extra-virgin olive oil

- 2 sliced scallions, white and green parts separated

- 4 cups sliced mixed mushrooms, wild, shiitake and/or white

- $\frac{1}{4}$ teaspoon salt

- $\frac{1}{2}$ teaspoons chopped fresh tarragon

INSTRUCTIONS

PREPARE STEAKS

a) Preheat oven to 425 degrees F.

b) Heat canola oil in a medium heavy oven-proof skillet. Meanwhile, sprinkle steaks with kosher salt and pepper. When oil shimmers, add steaks, and cook until the bottom is deeply browned, about 5 minutes. Turn steaks over, insert remote oven-proof inta-read thermometer into the center of one steak (if using) and transfer the skillet to the oven. Roast until the steaks are 130 degrees F for medium-rare 8 to 11 minutes. Transfer steaks to a plate and tent with foil to keep warm.

c) Place skillet over medium- high heat. Use caution the handle will be hot!! Add shallot and thyme to the skillet, and cook, stirring until the shallot is browned, about 30 seconds. Add vermouth and let simmer until almost reduced by one half. Stir the cornstarch into the broth and add to the skillet. Bring to a simmer, stirring. Cook until slightly thickened and reduced to about $\frac{1}{2}$ cup. Remove from the heat.

PREPARE TARRAGON MUSHROOMS.

d) Meanwhile while steaks roast, heat olive oil in a large skillet over medium-high heat. Add scallion whites, mushrooms and salt, and cook, stirring occasionally until the mushrooms are browning and the juices evaporate, 6 to 8 minutes. Stir in scallion greens and tarragon and remove from the heat.

e) Serve steaks with the vermouth sauce and mushrooms.

10. Slow cooker teriyaki salmon bowls

Ingredients

- 4 lemongrass stalks, bruised and cut into 4-inch pieces

- 1 fennel bulb (about 14 oz.), sliced

- 4 scallions, halved crosswise

- 1/3 cup water

- 1/3 cup dry white wine

- 1 (2-lb.) center-cut, skin-on salmon fillet

- 2 1/2 teaspoons kosher salt, divided

- 1 teaspoon black pepper, divided

- 12 ounces Brussels sprouts, quartered

- 2 tablespoons olive oil, divided

- 6 ounces shiitake mushroom caps, sliced

- 1/2 cup pineapple juice

- 2 tablespoons soy sauce

- 1 tablespoon brown sugar

- 1 teaspoon cornstarch

- 1 teaspoon sesame seeds

- 3 cups cooked brown rice

- 1 cup matchstick carrots

- Lime wedges, for serving

a) Fold a 30- x 18-inch piece of parchment paper in half lengthwise; fold in half again crosswise (short end to short end) to create a 4 layer thick piece. Place folded parchment in bottom of a 6-quart slow cooker, letting ends extend partially up sides.

b) Place half of lemongrass, fennel, and scallions in an even layer on parchment in slow cooker. Add water and wine. Sprinkle salmon with 1 teaspoon salt and 1/2 teaspoon pepper; place on lemongrass mixture.

Top salmon with remaining lemongrass, scallions, and fennel. Cover and cook on HIGH until salmon flakes easily with a fork, 1 to 2 hours. Using parchment paper liner as handles, lift salmon from slow cooker, allowing liquid to drain off. Discard mixture in slow cooker. Set salmon aside.

c) Preheat oven to 425°F. Toss Brussels sprouts with 1 tablespoon olive oil, 1 teaspoon kosher salt, and 1/2 teaspoon black pepper on a rimmed baking sheet. Bake in preheated oven until tender and starting to crisp, 20 to 25 minutes. Heat remaining 1 tablespoon olive oil in a skillet over medium-high and cook mushrooms and remaining 1/2 teaspoon kosher salt until tender, 3 to 4 minutes. Add mushrooms to baking sheet with Brussels sprouts; wipe skillet clean.

d) Cook pineapple juice, soy sauce, brown sugar, and cornstarch in skillet over medium, whisking constantly, until thickened, about 3 minutes. Brush 1/4 cup sauce on about 1 1/4 pounds cooked salmon; sprinkle with sesame seeds.

e) Place salmon on baking sheet with mushrooms and Brussels sprouts; broil on HIGH 6 inches from heat until glaze has thickened, about 2 minutes.

f) Divide brown rice among 4 bowls. Top evenly with salmon, Brussels sprouts, mushrooms, and matchstick carrots. Drizzle with remaining sauce; serve with lime wedges.

11. Maple roasted chicken quarters

INGREDIENTS

- 2 tablespoons olive oil

- 2 large chicken quarters or 4 chicken thighs, patted dry and rubbed with salt (kosher preferred)

- 2 carrots, peeled and cut into quarters

- 1 large potato, peeled and cut into cubes

- 1 small onion, sliced

- 6 cloves garlic, unpeeled

- 1 teaspoon salt (kosher preferred)

- 2 tablespoons pure maple syrup

- 1 tablespoon fresh thyme leaves

INSTRUCTIONS

a) Preheat oven to 425F/220C. Have a small casserole dish or an 8x8 pan ready.

b) In a large skillet over medium heat, heat 1 tablespoon oil. Once hot, add the chicken pieces, skin side down, and brown for 5 minutes. Flip and brown the other side for 5 minutes.

c) Meanwhile, in a large bowl add the carrots, potatoes, onion, and garlic and toss with the remaining 1 tablespoon oil and salt. Spread evenly into the bottom of the baking pan.

d) Once the chicken has finished browning, transfer chicken to sit on top of the vegetables, skin side up. Brush evenly with maple syrup and sprinkle with thyme.

e) Bake for 35-45 minutes or until internal temperature reaches 165F/74C. If the chicken is done before the vegetables, remove the chicken and cook the vegetables another 5-10 minutes or until softened.

12. Spinach and artichoke steak roll ups

INGREDIENTS

- 1 lb. flank steak

- 1 15.5-oz. can artichoke hearts, drained and chopped

- 2 c. baby spinach, chopped

- 2 cloves garlic, minced

- 1 c. ricotta

- 1/2 c. shredded white Cheddar

- kosher salt

- Freshly ground black pepper

DIRECTIONS

a) Preheat oven to 350°. On a cutting board, butterfly steak to make it a long rectangle that lays flat.

b) In a medium bowl, combine artichokes, spinach, garlic, ricotta, and cheddar and season generously with salt and pepper.

c) Spread steak with spinach-artichoke dip. Tightly roll up steak, then slice into rounds and bake until steak is cooked through to desired doneness, 23 to 25 minutes for medium. Serve with dressed greens.

13. Pasta with eggplant, burrata and mint

Ingredients

- 1/4 cup extra-virgin olive oil

- 1 tablespoon crushed red pepper

- 2 garlic cloves, thinly sliced

- 1 large eggplant, cut into 1-inch cubes (about 2 cups)

- 1 pound uncooked rigatoni, ziti, or orecchiette pasta

- 8 ounces fresh Burrata or mozzarella cheese

- 1/2 cup torn fresh mint, plus more for serving

- 1 teaspoon lemon zest, plus 1 Tbsp. fresh lemon juice (from 1 lemon)

a) Heat oil in a large skillet over medium. Add crushed red pepper and garlic; cook until fragrant, about 2 minutes. Add eggplant, and cook, stirring occasionally, until browned, about 20 minutes.

b) Meanwhile, cook pasta in boiling salted water according to package directions for al dente. Drain pasta, reserving 1 cup cooking water. Place cooked pasta in a serving bowl; add eggplant mixture. Slowly add reserved cooking water, tossing to coat. Tear fresh Burrata into pieces over the bowl (to catch any cream from the cheese), and add torn fresh mint, lemon zest, and lemon juice. Toss to combine. Add salt to taste, if desired. Top servings with additional mint.

14. Braised meatballs & mashed potatoes

Ingredients

For the meatballs

- 1 pound ground beef

- 1 pound ground pork

- 2 large eggs

- ½ cup plain bread crumbs

- ½ cup parmesan cheese grated

- 1 teaspoon salt

- $\frac{1}{2}$ teaspoon black pepper

- $\frac{1}{2}$ teaspoon crushed red pepper flakes

- $\frac{1}{4}$ cup fresh parsley chopped

- 1 tablespoon fresh oregano chopped

- 2 garlic cloves minced

- 3 tablespoons olive oil

For the gravy

- 1 medium shallot minced

- 2 garlic cloves minced

- 3 tablespoons flour

- 2 cups chicken or beef stock

- $\frac{1}{2}$ teaspoon salt

- $\frac{1}{2}$ teaspoon black pepper

- 2 teaspoons Worcestershire sauce

- For the roasted garlic mashed potatoes

- 4 large baking potatoes peeled and diced

- 5 tablespoons unsalted butter

- ¼ cup buttermilk

- 1 teaspoon salt

- ¾ teaspoon black pepper

- ½ cup parmesan cheese grated

- 8 garlic cloves peeled

- 1 tablespoon olive oil

For the roasted kale

- 4 cups fresh chopped kale

- 2 tablespoons olive oil

- ½ teaspoon salt

- ½ teaspoon black pepper

- ½ teaspoon crushed red pepper flakes

Instructions

a) Preheat oven to 375°F.

b) To make the meatballs, in a large bowl combine the ground meat, eggs, bread crumbs, parmesan cheese, salt, pepper, red pepper flakes, parsley, oregano and garlic. Stir with your hands until evenly combined. Form the meat into small balls the size of golf balls (but a little bit smaller). Heat a large heavy duty pot over medium high heat. Add the olive oil and sear the meatballs in batches. Cook for about 3 to 4 minutes on the first side, or until crispy and golden brown and then flip over and cook for another 2 to 3 minutes. Transfer to a plate and continue to cook the rest of the meatballs.

c) Once they've all been cooked, remove all but 1 tablespoon of olive oil from the pot. Add in the shallot and garlic and sauté for about 5 minutes or until soft. Stir in the flour and cook for a minute. Slowly stream in, while whisking constantly, the chicken stock until the roux has dissolved completely. Lower the heat and cook until bubbly and thick. Season with a salt, pepper, and Worcestershire sauce. Lower the flame to as low as it'll go and return the meatballs to the pot, nestling them into the gravy. Simmer for about 15 to 20 minutes, semi-covered with a lid.

d) To make the potatoes, wrap the garlic cloves in foil with the olive oil and a pinch of salt and black pepper. Roast in the oven for about 20 to 25 minutes. Place the potatoes in a medium pot and cover with cold water. Bring to a boil and cook for about 15 to 20 minutes or until fork tender. Drain and return to pot. Add in the butter, buttermilk, salt, pepper, roasted garlic, and parmesan. Mash until smooth. Keep warm on the stove over low heat.

e)   To make the kale, place the kale on a baking sheet and toss with olive oil, salt, pepper, and red pepper flakes. Spread out onto an even layer and roast for about 10 to 15 minutes or until charred and crispy.

f)   To serve, spoon the potatoes onto the plates and top with the roasted kale. Place a few meatballs on top of the kale and spoon over with gravy. Garnish with chopped fresh parsley on top. Enjoy!

15. Engagement chicken pasta

Ingredients

- 6 ounces dried spaghetti

- 4 tablespoons unsalted butter

- 10 sprigs fresh thyme

- 10 ounces sliced mushrooms

- freshly ground black pepper

- salt

- 2 small chicken breasts

- 2 teaspoons olive oil

- 1/2 cup dry white wine

- 4 ounces cream cheese, softened

Instructions

a) Bring a large pot of salted water to a boil, and cook the spaghetti noodles.

b) Meanwhile, in a large not non-stick skillet, melt the butter and thyme over medium heat.

c) Add the sliced mushrooms to the skillet, and stir to coat in butter. Leave them to cook for a few minutes undisturbed so that a nice crust forms. Stir, and repeat until the mushrooms are golden brown. It will take about 15 minutes.

d) Using a slotted spoon, remove the mushrooms from the pan, leaving the butter and thyme in the pan. Add the oil to the pan.

e) Salt and pepper both sides of the chicken breasts.

f) Turn the heat up to medium-high, and sear the chicken breasts on both sides in the same pan that the mushrooms were in. Again, let cook undisturbed so that a nice crust forms. If the chicken is sticking to the pan, it's because the first side isn't done searing. It will release when it's golden brown.

g) Remove the chicken from the pan, and cover to keep warm.

h) Turn the heat down to low and add all of the wine

i) Allow the wine to cook down slightly while scraping the bottom of the pan with a wooden spoon to get all of the brown bits into the wine.

j) Dice the cream cheese and place in a large bowl.

k) Discard the thyme sprigs from the pan, and then pour the hot wine over the cream cheese, and stir until it melts. There might be a few small pieces, but the hot pasta will dissolve them.

l) When the pasta is done, drain it, and immediately pour it over the wine-cream cheese mixture. Toss the noodles to melt and evenly distribute the cream cheese sauce.

m) Stir the mushrooms into the pasta bowl.

n) Slice the chicken, and serve on top.

16. Surf and turf for two

INGREDIENTS

serves 2

For the steaks and seasoning:

- 2, 8oz filet mignon steaks, cut 2" thick

- 3/4 Tablespoon rock salt

- 1-1/2 teaspoons black peppercorns

- 1/2 teaspoon dried minced garlic

- 1/2 teaspoon dried minced onion

- big pinch fennel seeds

- small pinch red chili pepper flakes

- drizzle extra virgin olive oil

- 2 Tablespoons butter

For the pan sauce:

- 1 Tablespoon minced shallot

- 1 garlic clove, crushed and peeled

- 1 sprig fresh rosemary

- 1/2 cup red wine, like cabernet

- 1 cup low-sodium beef broth

- 1 Tablespoon butter

- For the scallops:

- 1 Tablespoon butter

- 1 Tablespoon extra virgin olive oil

- 6 large sea scallops

- salt and pepper

DIRECTIONS

a) Place steak on a plate on the counter to warm up for about 30 minutes before starting to cook. Preheat oven to 400 degrees.

b) For the steaks: Add rock salt, peppercorns, dried garlic, dried onion, fennel, and red chili pepper flakes to a mortar and pestle then coarsely crush seasonings. Alternatively you could use a spice grinder or use your favorite store-bought steak rub instead. Drizzle tops of steaks with extra virgin olive oil then generously sprinkle on spice rub and rub into steaks. Repeat on the other side.

c) Heat a large, oven-safe cast iron or heavy-bottomed skillet over medium-high heat until very hot then add butter. Once melted, add steaks then sear until a golden brown crust has formed on the bottom, 2 minutes. Flip steaks then place entire skillet into oven and roast for 10 minutes for medium doneness (adjust roasting time up or down depending on how thick your steaks are - ours were 2" thick.) Remove steaks to a plate to rest while you prepare the rest of the dish.

d) For the pan sauce: Place hot skillet back over medium-high heat then add shallots and saute for 30 seconds. Add rosemary, garlic, and wine then simmer until wine is reduced by half. Add beef broth then simmer until sauce is thickened and reduced, 7-9 minutes. Add butter, taste then add salt and pepper if necessary, and then set aside.

e) For the scallops: Pat scallops very dry between layers of paper towels then season with salt and pepper on both sides. Melt butter and extra virgin olive oil in a large skillet over medium-high heat then add scallops and sear for 90 seconds. Flip then sear for 90 more seconds.

f) Plate steaks and scallops on two plates then drizzle pan sauce over steaks and serve.

17. Lobster noodle casserole

INGREDIENTS

- 2 fresh lobsters

- 3 tbsp. salt

- 1/2 tsp. salt

- 3 tbsp. butter

- 1 shallot

- 1 tbsp. tomato paste

- 3 clove garlic

- 1/4 c. brandy

- 1/2 c. heavy cream

- tsp. fresh-ground black pepper

- 1/2 lb. egg noodles

- 1 tbsp. fresh lemon juice

- 6 sprig thyme

DIRECTIONS

a) Cook the lobsters:

b) Fill a large bowl halfway with ice and water and set aside. Bring a large pot of water and 3 tablespoons of the salt to a boil and plunge the lobsters, headfirst, into the water with long-handled tongs. Reduce heat to low and cook, covered, for 4 minutes. Drain the lobsters and place in the prepared ice bath to cool. Crack the shells and remove the tail and claw meat. Reserve the shells. Cut the tail meat into 1/2-inch-thick medallions and the claw meat into large pieces and set aside.

c) Bake the casseroles:

d) Preheat oven to 350°F. Lightly coat four 1-cup-capacity baking dishes or one 9-inch round baking dish with 1 tablespoon butter and set aside. Melt the remaining butter in a medium skillet over medium heat. Add the shallot and cook until soft. Add the reserved shells, tomato paste, and garlic and cook, stirring continuously, for 5 minutes. Move the pan away from the heat and add the brandy. Return to the heat and bring the mixture to a boil, whisking continuously. Reduce heat to medium low, add 1 1/2 cups water, and simmer until thickened slightly -- about 15 minutes. Strain the mixture and stir in the cream, remaining salt, and pepper. Add the egg noodles, lobster meat, and lemon juice and toss to coat. Divide the mixture evenly among the prepared baking dishes, cover with foil, and bake until the lobster is cooked through and the noodles are hot -- about 20 minutes. Garnish with thyme sprigs and serve immediately.

18. Risotto with chicken and spring peas

Ingredients

- 1 tablespoon olive oil

- $\frac{1}{4}$ cup chopped onion

- 1 clove garlic, minced

- $\frac{1}{2}$ cup uncooked arborio rice

- 2 $\frac{1}{4}$ cups chicken or vegetable broth

- $\frac{1}{2}$ cup loose-pack frozen tiny or regular-size peas

- 2 tablespoons coarsely shredded carrot

- ⅔ cup shredded cooked chicken

- 1 cup fresh spinach, shredded

- 2 tablespoons grated Parmesan cheese (1 ounce)

- 1 teaspoon snipped fresh thyme

a) In a large saucepan heat oil over medium heat. Add onion and garlic; cook until onion is tender. Add the uncooked rice. Cook and stir about 5 minutes or until rice is golden brown.

b) Meanwhile, in a medium saucepan bring broth to boiling; reduce heat to keep broth simmering. Carefully add 1/2 cup of the broth to the rice mixture, stirring constantly. Continue to cook and stir over medium heat until liquid is absorbed. Add another 1/2 cup of the broth to the rice mixture, stirring constantly. Continue to cook and stir until liquid is absorbed. Add another 1/2 cup broth, 1/4 cup at a time, stirring constantly until the broth has been absorbed. (This should take 18 to 20 minutes total.)

c) Stir in remaining broth, the peas, and carrot. Cook and stir until rice is slightly firm (al dente) and creamy.

d) Stir in chicken, spinach, Parmesan cheese, and thyme; heat through. Serve immediately.

19. Mustard crusted lamb

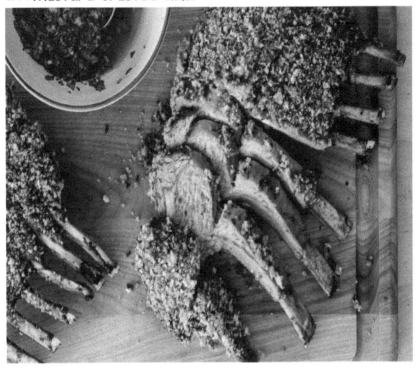

INGREDIENTS

- 1 New Zealand lamb rib roast (rack of lamb), 8 ribs

- salt and pepper

- 3 tbsp. Dijon mustard with seeds

- 2 tbsp. chopped fresh mint or basil leaves

- 4 tbsp. chopped shallots

- 1/4 c. panko (Japanese bread crumbs)

- 3 small red potatoes

- 2 tbsp. water

- 1/2 bunch broccoli rabe

- 1 tsp. olive oil

- 3 tbsp. reduced-fat sour cream

a) Preheat oven to 425 degrees. Place lamb, meat side up, in small roasting pan. Sprinkle lamb with 1/4 teaspoon each salt and freshly ground black pepper. In small bowl, stir together mustard, mint, and 2 tablespoons shallots. Reserve 2 tablespoons mustard mixture for sauce; spread remainder on lamb. Pat on panko to coat.

b) Roast lamb in oven 25 to 30 minutes for medium-rare (140 degrees on meat thermometer) or until desired doneness.

c) Meanwhile, heat 4-quart saucepan of water to boiling on high. In microwave-safe medium bowl, combine potatoes and 2 tablespoons cold water. Cover with vented plastic wrap, and microwave on High 4 minutes or until fork-tender. Drain; toss with 1/8 teaspoon each salt and freshly ground black pepper. Keep warm.

d) Add broccoli rabe to boiling water in saucepan, and cook 3 minutes. Drain well; wipe pan dry. In same saucepan, heat oil and remaining 2 tablespoons shallots on medium-high; add broccoli rabe and cook 2 minutes, stirring frequently. Toss with 1/8 teaspoon each salt and freshly ground black pepper. Keep warm.

e) Stir sour cream into reserved mustard mixture. Cut lamb into 2-rib portions, and place on 2 dinner plates with potatoes and broccoli rabe. Serve lamb with sour cream sauce.

20. Proscuitto and arugula pizza

INGREDIENTS

- 1 pound pizza dough, at room temperature, divided into 2 equal pieces

- 2 tablespoons olive oil

- 1/2 cup tomato sauce

- 1 1/2 cups shredded mozzarella cheese (6 ounces)

- 8 thin slices prosciutto

- A few big handfuls of arugula

INSTRUCTIONS

a) If you have a pizza stone, place it on a rack in the middle of the oven. Heat the oven to 550°F (or maximum oven temperature) for at least 30 minutes.

b) If transferring the pizza to a stone in the oven, assemble on a well-floured peel or cutting board. Otherwise, assemble on the surface you will be cooking on (parchment paper, baking sheet, etc.). Working with one piece of dough at a time, roll or stretch it into a 10- to 12-inch circle. Brush the edges of the dough with 1 tablespoon of olive oil. Spread half of the tomato sauce over the rest of the dough. Sprinkle with about a 1/4 of the cheese. Lay 4 prosciutto slices so they are evenly covering the dough. Sprinkle with another 1/4 of the cheese.

c) Bake the pizza until edges are lightly browned and cheese is bubbly and browned in spots, about 6 minutes at 550°F. Remove from oven to a cutting board, scatter half of the arugula over the top, and cut and serve immediately. Repeat with the remaining dough and toppings.

21. Chicken, shrimp & chorizo paella

Ingredients

- ½ teaspoon saffron threads, crushed

- 2 tablespoons olive oil

- 1 pound skinless, boneless chicken thighs, cut into 2-inch pieces

- 4 ounces cooked, smoked Spanish-style chorizo sausage, sliced

- 1 medium onion, chopped

- 4 cloves garlic, minced

- 1 cup coarsely grated tomatoes (about 1 pound)*

- 1 tablespoon smoked sweet paprika

- 6 cups reduced-sodium chicken broth

- 2 cups short grain Spanish rice, such as bomba, Calasparra, or Valencia

- 12 large shrimp, peeled and deveined

- 8 ounces frozen peas, thawed

- Chopped green olives (optional)

- Chopped Italian parsley

a) In a small bowl combine saffron and 1/4 cup hot water; let stand 10 minutes.

b) Meanwhile, in a 15-inch paella pan heat oil over medium-high heat. Add chicken to pan. Cook, turning occasionally, until chicken is browned, about 5 minutes. Add chorizo. Cook 1 minute more. Transfer all to a plate. Add onion and garlic to pan. Cook and stir 2 minutes. Add tomatoes and paprika. Cook and stir 5 minutes more or until tomatoes are thickened and almost pastelike.

c) Return chicken and chorizo to pan. Add chicken broth, saffron mixture, and 1/2 tsp. salt; bring to boiling over high heat. Add rice to pan, stirring once to evenly distribute. Cook, without stirring, until rice has absorbed most of the liquid, about 12 minutes. (If your pan is bigger than your burner, rotate every few minutes to ensure the rice cooks evenly.) Reduce heat to low. Cook, without stirring, 5 to 10 minutes more until all the liquid is absorbed and rice is al dente. Top with shrimp and peas. Turn heat to high. Cook without stirring, 1 to 2 minutes more (edges should look dry and a crust should form on the bottom). Remove. Cover pan with foil. Let rest 10 minutes before serving. Top with olives, if desired, and parsley.

22. Tarragon Lamb

- 4 lb leg of lamb
- 1 ts tarragon
- 1 tb oil
- 1 ea onion, sliced
- 1 1/4 c dry white wine
- 1 x salt and pepper to taste
- 2/3 c cream

a) Skin the leg of lamb and trim away all the outside fat.

b) Score the flesh deeply with a criss-cross pattern and stuff the slits with the tarragon. Rub the meat with the oil and cover with the onion.

c) Place in a suitable dish for marinating and pour the white wine over top.

d) Add salt and pepper to taste and marinate for about 2 hours, basting occasionally.

e) Roast the lamb with the marinade, at 325 degrees F. until done; baste frequently.

f) Ten minutes before the meat is finished cooking, pour off the marinade and meat juices into a saucepan.

g) Reduce the gravy to half its original quantity by boiling vigorously.

h) Carve the meat into thin slices and add the juices from the meat to the marinade.

i) Arrange the meat on a a serving dish and keep warm.

Remove the gravy from the heat, stir in the cream and slowly reheat until it forms a medium-thick consistency. Pour the sauce over the lamb and keep warm till ready to serve.

23. Spanish Rice with Beef

- 1 lb Lean Ground Beef

- 1/2 c Onion; Chopped, 1 Md

- 1 c Rice; Regular, Uncooked

- 2/3 c Green Bell Pepper; Chopped

- 16 oz Stewed Tomatoes; 1 Cn

- 5 ea Bacon Slices; Crisp,Crumbled

- 2 c Water

- 1 ts Chili Powder

- 1/2 ts Oregano

- 1 1/4 ts Salt

- 1/8 ts Pepper

a) Cook and stir the meat and onion in a large skillet until the meat is brown. Drain off the excess fat.

b) Stir in the rice, green pepper, tomatoes, bacon, water, chili powder, oregano, salt and pepper.

c) To Cook in a Skillet:

d) Heat the mixture to boiling then reduce the heat and simmer, covered, stirring occasionally, until the rice is tender, about 30 minutes. (A small amount of water can be added if necessary.)

e) To Cook in the Oven:

f) Pour the mixture into an ungreased 2-quart casserole.

g) Cover and bake at 375 degrees F, stirring occasionally, until the rice is tender, about 45 minutes.

h) Serve hot.

24. Chicken Parmesan

- 1/2 c Fine, dry bread crumbs

- 1/4 c Grated Parmesan cheese

- 4 ea Chicken breasts, boneless

- 1 ea Egg, beaten

- 3 tb Butter

- 1 ea 8 oz. can tomato sauce
- 1/2 c Water
- 1/4 ts Dried whole oregano 1 c Shredded mozzarella cheese

a) Combine bread crumbs and parmesan cheese.

b) Dip chicken in egg and coat well.

c) Preheat skillet to 350 degrees.

d) Add butter and cook chicken for about 3 minutes on each side.

e) Combine the tomato sauce, water, and oregano; pour over chicken.

f) Reduce heat to 220 degrees, cover and cook 25-30 minutes.

g) Sprinkle with mozzerella cheese; cover and cook just until cheese melts.

25. Salmon Steaks with White Wine Sauce

- 8 oz (2) Salmon Steaks *

- 2 ts Cooking Oil White Wine Sauce:

- 1 tb Butter or Margarine

- 1 ts Cornstarch

- 1 x Dash White Pepper

- 1/2 c Half Half Light Cream

- 1 ea Lge. Beaten Egg Yolk

- 2 tb Dry White Wine

- 1 x Seedless Green Grapes (Opt.)

a) Preheat a 6 1/2-inch microwave browning dish on 100% power for 3 minutes. Add cooking oil to the browning dish; swirl to coat the dish.

b) Place salmon steaks in the browning dish. Microwave, covered, on

c) 100% power for about 30 seconds. Turn the salmon steaks and

d) microwave, covered, on 50% power about 3 minutes or until the salmon flakes easily when tested with a fork.

e) Let salmon steaks stand, covered, while preparing the wine sauce.

f) For the wine sauce: In a 4-cup measure microwave the butter or margarine, uncovered, on 100% of power for 45 seconds to 1 minute or until melted. Stir in the cornstarch and white pepper. Stir in light cream.

g) Microwave, uncovered, on 100% power for 2 to 3 minutes or until mixture is thickened and bubbly, stirring every minute.

h) Stir half the hot cream mixture into the beaten egg yolk.

i) Return all to the 4-cup measure. Microwave, uncovered, on 50% power for 1 minute, stirring every 15 seconds until mixture is smooth. Stir in dry white wine.

j) Transfer the salmon steaks to a serving platter and spoon the wine sauce over top. Garnish with seedless green grapes, if desired.

26. Fettuccine with Cream, Basil and Romano

- 4 ea Bacon slices; chopped thick

- 4 ea Green onions; chopped

- 1/2 c Whipping cream

- 1/2 c Parmesan; freshly grated

- 1/3 c Basil; chopped fresh

- 1/2 lb Fettuccine

- 1 x Salt and pepper

- 1 x Parmesan; freshly grated

a) Cook bacon in heavy medium skillet over medium heat until beginning to brown. Add green onions and stir until softened, about 1 minute. Add cream and simmer until beginning to thicken, about 1 minute. Mix in parmesan cheese and basil.

b) Meanwhile, cook fettuccine in large pot of boiling, salted water until just tender but still firm to the bite (al dente), stirring occasionally. Drain well.

c) Return to hot pot. Add sauce and stir to coat. Season with salt and pepper.

d) Serve immediately; pass the grated parmesan.

27. Crispy Chicken Drumsticks

- 8 x Chicken Drumsticks, skinned *
- 1 1/2 c Breadcrumbs
- 1/4 c Grated Parmesan Cheese
- 2 tb Minced fresh Parsley
- 1/4 ts Garlic powder
- Salt and Pepper to taste
- 1/3 c Skim Milk

a) Rinse chicken with cold water, and pat dry.

b) Combine bread crumbs, parmesan cheese, parsley, garlic powder, salt and pepper; stir well.

c) Dip drumsticks in skim milk then dredge in breadcrumb mixture, coating well.

d) Place drumsticks in a 10x6x2 inch baking dish sprayed with Pam.

e) Bake at 350 degrees F. for 1 hour.

28. Salmon Steaks with Cucumber Dill Sauce

- 2 ea Salmon steaks

- 1/4 c Dry white wine

- 1 ea Bay leaf

- 2 tb Fresh dill

- 1 ea Stalk celery, cut up Cucumber Dill Sauce:

- 1/4 c Plain low-fat yogurt

- 1/4 c Lite mayonnaise

- 1 ea Small seeded grated cucumber
- 1 ea Small onion, peeled grated
- 1/8 ts Dry mustard
- 1/4 c Freshly chopped dill
- Salt and pepper to taste

a) Place steaks in microwave safe dish w/ thick end to outside. Mix together the white wine, bay leaf, dill, and celery; spread mixture evenly over the salmon steaks.

b) Cover and microwave on high for 4-6 minutes.

c) Serve with cucumber-dill sauce.

d) For Cucumber-Dill Sauce:

e) Combine the yogurt, mayonnaise, cucumber, onion, mustard, dill, salt and pepper in a food processor and blend well.

f) Pour into serving bowl; refrigerate for 1 to 2 hours before serving.

29. Turkey Taco Salad

- 3 ea flour tortillas*
- 1/2 lb ground turkey
- 1/3 c water
- 1 ts chili powder
- 1/2 ts salt

- 1/4 ts garlic powder
- 1/4 ts cayenne pepper
- 8 oz kidney beans, drained
- 5 c shredded lettuce
- 1 ea medium tomato, chopped
- 1/2 c shredded Monterey Jack cheese
- 1/4 c onion, chopped
- 1/4 c Thousand Island dressing
- 1/4 c sour cream (garnish)
- 4 ea pitted ripe olives, sliced (garnish)

a) Preheat oven to 400 degrees F.

b) Cut tortillas into 12 wedges or 3x1/4-inch strips and place in a 15 1/2 x 10 1/2 x 1 inch ungreased jelly roll pan.

c) Bake 6 to 8 minutes, stirring at least once, until golden brown and crisp; cool.

d) Cook ground turkey in non-stick skillet, stirring frequently, until browned. Stir in water, chili powder, salt, garlic powder, red pepper,

e) and kidney beans. Heat to boiling; reduce heat. Simmer uncovered 2 to 3 minutes, stirring occasionally, until liquid is absorbed.

f) Cool 10 minutes.

g) Mix lettuce, tomato, cheese, onion in a large bowl; toss with the

h) Thousand Island dressing; divide between 4 dinner plates. Top each salad with about 1/2 cup turkey mixture.

i) Arrange tortilla wedges around salad and garnish with sour cream and olives.

30. Cornish Game Hen with Kasha Stuffing

Categories: Main dish, Poultry

- 2   ea Rock Cornish game hens

- 1/2 ea lemon

- Salt and pepper

- 4 ea strips bacon   3/4 c red wine Kasha Stuffing:

- 1 c buckwheat groats

- 1   ea egg (slightly beaten)

- 2   c boiling water

- 3   ea strips bacon (cut in pieces)

- 4   tb butter

- 1 ea medium onion (chopped)

- 1 ea clove garlic (minced)

- 1/2 ea green pepper (chopped)

- 1/4 lb mushrooms (chopped)

- 1 ts oregano

- 1/2 ts sage

- Salt and pepper to taste

a) Rub birds inside and out with lemon and sprinkle well with salt and freshly ground pepper.

b) Preheat oven (450 degrees F.).

c) Fill cavities with the Kasha stuffing. Close opening with skewers.

d) Place birds, breast side up, on rack in open roasting pan and cover breasts with bacon. Cool for 15 minutes.

e) Reduce heat to 325 degrees F. and add red wine. Roast for 35 to 40 minutes, basting often (like every 15 minutes, if possible); add more wine if necessary.

f) For Kasha Stuffing:

g) Mix the groats with beaten egg; add to frying pan over high heat. Stir constantly until grains separate, then add the boiling water.

h) Cover pan, reduce heat, and simmer for 30 minutes.

i) Meanwhile, fry the bacon in another large frying pan.

j) When bacon is lightly browned, push to one side and add the butter.

k) Let this sizzle and add onion, garlic , green pepper, and mushrooms; stir constantly.

l) Add oregano, sage, and salt and pepper. Reduce heat and add the cooked groats. Mix well, adjust seasoning, and remove from heat.

m) Kasha is frequently called buckwheat groats. It is made from buckwheat grain and then roasted, which gives it a delicious nut-like flavor.

n) Aside from being a tasty stuffing for poultry, this recipe makes an excellent side dish in place of rice, potatoes, or noodles.

ROMANTIC SALADS

31. Romance-in-a-Bowl Salad

Ingredient

- 4 cups baby salad greens

- 1 carrot, peeled and sliced

- 2 green onions, chopped

- 6 strawberries, hulled and sliced

- 12 fresh raspberries

- 1 teaspoon minced garlic

- $\frac{1}{4}$ cup chopped walnuts

- $\frac{1}{4}$ cup seasoned almond slices

- $\frac{1}{4}$ cup dried currants

- $\frac{1}{4}$ cup crumbled feta cheese

- $\frac{1}{2}$ cup seasoned croutons

- $\frac{1}{2}$ cup herbed vinaigrette salad dressing, or to taste

a) In a large bowl, toss together the salad greens, carrot, green onions, strawberries, raspberries, garlic, walnuts, almond slices, currants and feta cheese. Divide between two salad bowls. Top each bowl with some croutons and serve with vinaigrette dressing.

32. Pink Salad

Ingredients

Salad

- 4 whole carrots, I used purple

- 1/3 medium red onion, slivered

- 1 large beet

- 1 pink grapefruit, sectioned
- 1 handful roughly chopped pistachios

Vinaigrette

- 1/2 cup olive oil
- 1/4 cup rice wine vinegar
- 1 tsp mustard
- 1 tsp maple syrup
- 1-2 cloves garlic, minced
- salt and pepper to taste

Instructions

a) Slice your beets into medium wedges and place in a microwaveable container, cover and micro until fork tender. Mine took 6 1/2 minutes. I choose not to peel mine as I don't mind the skin but do what you like.

b) Using a carrot peeler shave off long strips from each carrot until you reach the core and can shave no more. Save the cores for munching on later.

c) In a large bowl place all of your salad ingredients except the pistachios.

d) In another bowl place all of the dressing ingredients and whisk until emulsified.

e) When you are ready to serve the salad toss with enough dressing to coat and reserve the rest for tomorrow's salad. Note if you make the salad and dress it in advance the beets will "bleed " all over the salad and it will end up a monochromatic red.

f) Sprinkle on the pistachios and you are good to go.

33. Mixed green spring salad

- 2 OZ. Mixed Greens
- 3 tbsp. Pine Nuts, roasted
- 2 tbsp. 5 Minute Raspberry Vinaigrette
- 2 tbsp. Shaved Parmesan
- 2 slices Bacon
- Salt and Pepper to taste

1. Cook bacon until very crisp. I let mine slightly burn on the edges to give the salad a slight addition in bitter notes in some bites.
2. Measure out your greens and set in a container that can be shaken.

3.Crumble bacon, then add the rest of the ingredients to the greens. Shake the container with a lid on to distribute the dressing and contents evenly.
4.Serve and enjoy!

Crispy tofu and bok choy salad

Oven Baked Tofu
- 15 oz. Extra Firm Tofu
- 1 tbsp. Soy Sauce
- 1 tbsp. Sesame Oil
- 1 tbsp. Water
- 2 tsp. Minced Garlic
- 1 tbsp. Rice Wine Vinegar
- Juice 1/2 Lemon

Bok Choy Salad
- 9 oz. Bok Choy
- 1 stalk Green Onion
- 2 tbsp. Cilantro, chopped
- 3 tbsp. Coconut Oil
- 2 tbsp. Soy Sauce
- 1 tbsp. Sambal Olek

- 1 tbsp. Peanut Butter
- Juice 1/2 lime
- 7 drops Liquid Stevia

1. Start by pressing the tofu. Lay the tofu in a kitchen towel and put something heavy over the top (like a cast iron skillet). It takes about 4-6 hours to dry out, and you may need to replace the kitchen towel half-way through.
2. Once the tofu is pressed, work on your marinade. Combine all of the ingredients for the marinade (soy sauce, sesame oil, water, garlic, vinegar, and lemon).
3. Chop the tofu into squares and place in a plastic bag along with the marinade. Let this marinate for at least 30 minutes, but preferably over night.
4. Pre-heat oven to 350F. Place tofu on a baking sheet lined with parchment paper (or a silpat) and bake for 30-35 minutes.
5. As the tofu is cooked, get started on the bok choy salad. Chop cilantro and spring onion.
6. Mix all of the other ingredients together (except lime juice and bok choy) in
a bowl. Then add cilantro and spring onion. Note: You can microwave coconut oil for 10-15 seconds to allow it to melt.
7. Once the tofu is almost cooked, add lime juice into the salad dressing and mix together.
8. Chop the bok choy into small slices, like you would cabbage.
9. Remove the tofu from the oven and assemble your salad with tofu, bokchoy, and sauce.

34. Bbq pork salad

The Salad
- 10 oz. Pulled Pork
- 2 cups Romaine Lettuce
- 1/4 cup Cilantro, chopped
- 1/4 medium Red Bell Pepper, Chopped

The Sauce
- 2 tbsp. Tomato Paste
- 2 tbsp. + 2 tsp. Soy Sauce (or coconut aminos)
- 1 tbsp. Creamy Peanut Butter
- 2 tbsp. Cilantro, chopped
- Juice & Zest of 1/2 Lime
- 1 tsp. Five Spice
- 1 tsp. Red Curry Paste
- 1 tbsp. + 1 tsp. Rice Wine Vinegar
- 1/4 tsp. Red Pepper Flakes

- 1 tsp. Fish Sauce/10 drops Liquid Stevia AND 1/2 tsp. Mango Extract

1. In a bowl, combine all the sauce ingredients together (except for cilantro and lime zest).
2. Chop cilantro and zest a lime and add to the sauce.
3. Mix the Thai BBQ sauce together well, and then set aside. Using your fingers, or a knife, pull apart the pork. Assemble the salad and glaze over the pork with some sauce.

35. Red pepper spinach salad

- 6 Cups Spinach
- 1/4 Cup Ranch Dressing
- 3 Tbsp. Parmesan Cheese
- 1 tsp. Red Pepper Flakes

1. In a large mixing bowl, measure out 6 Cup of Spinach.
2. Add 1/4 Cup Ranch Dressing and mix it into the spinach. Then, add 3 Tbsp.
Parmesan Cheese and 1 tsp. Red Pepper Flakes. Mix well again

36. Spinach Pecan Salad

- 2 pounds fresh spi nach
- Salt or Vege-Sal
- 10 scallions, thinly sliced, including about 2 inches of the green sprout
- 1/4 cup extra-virgin olive oil
- 1/4 cup lemon juice
- 1/4 pound toasted, salted pecans, chopped

1. Wash and dry the spinach until you're absolutely sure it's clean-spinach can hold a lot of grit! When you're sure it's clean and dry, put it in a salad bowl, and sprinkle it with a little salt-maybe a teaspoonful-and

squeeze the leaves gently with your hands. You'll find that the spinach "deflates," or sort of gets a bit limp and reduces in volume. Add the scallions to the bowl.

2. Pour on the olive oil, and toss the salad thoroughly. Add the lemon juice, and toss again. Top with the pecans, and serve.

37. Update Salad

Salad

- 2 medium green peppers, cut in smallish strips
- 1 large bunch parsley, chopped
- 2/3 cup torn radicchio
- 2/3 cup chopped curly endive
- 2/3 cup chopped frizee
- 3 tomatoes, each cut in 8 lengthwise wedges
- 1/8 of a large, sweet red onion, thinly sliced
- 2 tablespoons chopped black olives

Dressing

- 1/4 cup water
- 1/2 cup tarragon vinegar
- 1/2 teaspoon salt or Vege-Sal
- 1 1/2 tablespoons lemon juice

- 1 tablespoon Splenda
- 1/8 teaspoon blackstrap molasses

1. Put the peppers, parsl, radicchio, endive, frizee, tomatoes, onion, and olives in a big bowl, and set aside.
2. In a separate bowl, combine the water, vinegar, salt, lemon juice, Splenda, and molasses. Pour it all over the salad, and toss.
3. Stick the whole thing in the refrigerator, and let it sit there for a few hours, stirring it now and then if you think of it.

38. California Salad

- 4 cups torn romaine lettuce
- 4 cups torn red leaf lettuce
- 1 ripe, black avocado
- 3 tablespoons extra-virgin olive oil
- 2 tablespoons lemon juice
- Salt and pepper
- 1/2 cup alfalfa sprouts

1. Combine the romaine and red leaf lettuces in a salad bowl, then peel the avocado and cut it into small chunks. (It's easiest just to scoop out bits with a spoon.) Add the avocado to the bowl.
2. Toss the salad first with the oil, then the lemon juice, then finally with salt and pepper to taste. Top with the sprouts, and serve.

39. Melon Prosciutto Salad

- 1/2 ripe cantaloupe
- 1/2 ripe hondew
- 8 ounces prosciutto

1. Seed and peel the melons, and cut them into 1-inch chunks (or use a melon bailer).
2. Chop the prosciutto, toss everything together, and serve.

Gorkensalad

- 4 peeled cucumbers, thinly sliced
- 1 1/2 tablespoons salt
- 1/4 cup water
- 3 tablespoons cider vinegar
- 3 tablespoons oil
- 2 tablespoons Splenda
- Pepper

1. Peel and slice the cucumbers. Put them in a large bowl and sprinkle the salt over them. Stir the salt into the cucumbers, cover, and refrigerate overnight.
2. An hour or so before serving, remove the cucumbers from the refrigerator and squeeze the water out of them, using your hands and working in small batches. The

slices will go from kind of stiff and opaque to limp and almost translucent. Pour off the resulting water.

3. Mix together the water, vinegar, oil, and Splenda, and salt and pepper to taste. This is the "dressing"-it should be light, tangy, and just slightly sweet. Pour this over the cucumbers, and mix them up. Chill until ready to serve.

40. Colorful Bean Salad

- 1 can (14 1/2 ounces) cut green beans
- 1 can (14 1/2 ounces) cut wax beans
- 1/2 cup chopped sweet red onion
- 3/4 cup Splenda
- 1 teaspoon salt
- 1/2 teaspoon pepper
- 1/2 cup canola oil
- 2/3 cup cider vinegar

1. Drain the green and wax beans, and combine them in a bowl with the onion.
2. In a separate bowl, combine the Splenda, salt, pepper, oil, and vinegar; pour the mixture over the vegetables.
3. Let it marinate for several hours at least; overnight won't hurt. Drain off the marinade, and serve.

41. Coleslaw for Two

- 1 head red cabbage
- 1 small carrot, shredded
- 1/4 sweet red onion, finely minced
- Coleslaw Dressing

1. Using a food processor's slicing blade or a sharp knife, shred your cabbage and put it in a big bowl.
2. Add the carrot and onion, and toss with the dressing. Admire, and enjoy.

Confetti UnSlaw

- 2 cups shredded green cabbage
- 2 cups shredded red cabbage
- 1/2 sweet red pepper, chopped
- 1/2 green pepper, chopped
- 4 scallions, sliced, including the crisp part of the green
- 1/3 CU P grated ca rrat
- 1 small celery rib, thinly sliced
- 2 tablespoons minced fresh parsley

Mix

43. Caponata Salad

- 1/4 cup olive oil
- medium eggplant, peeled and cut into 1/4-inch dice
- small red onion, chopped
- celery rib, chopped
- 2 garlic cloves, minced
- 2 cups chopped fresh or drained canned plum tomatoes
- 2 tablespoons capers
- 3 tablespoons red wine vinegar
- 2 teaspoons sugar
- 1 tablespoon minced fresh basil or 1 teaspoon dried
- 1/2 teaspoon salt

In a large saucepan, heat the oil over medium heat. Add the eggplant, onion, celery, and garlic. Cover and cook until the vegetables are softened, about 15 minutes. Add the tomatoes, cover, and cook 5 minutes longer. Stir in the capers, vinegar, sugar, basil, and salt and simmer, uncovered, for 5 minutes to allow flavors to develop.

Remove from heat and allow to cool slightly, then transfer to a large bowl and refrigerate until chilled, about 2 hours. Taste, adjusting seasonings if necessary. Serve chilled or at room temperature.

44. Green Bean And Pear Salad

- 1/4 cup toasted sesame oil
- 3 tablespoons rice vinegar
- 2 tablespoons almond butter
- 2 tablespoons soy sauce
- 1 tablespoon agave nectar
- 1 teaspoon grated fresh ginger
- 1/8 teaspoon ground cayenne
- 8 ounces green beans, trimmed and cut into 1-inch pieces
- 1/4 cup minced red onion
- 2 ripe pears, cored and cut into 1/2-inch dice
- 1/4 cup golden raisins
- 4 to 6 cups mixed salad greens

In a blender or food processor, combine the oil, vinegar, almond butter, soy sauce, agave nectar, ginger, and cayenne. Process to blend. Set aside.

In a saucepan of boiling water, immerse the green beans and carrot and cook until crisp-tender, about 5 minutes. Drain and transfer to a large bowl. Add the onion, pears, almonds, and raisins. Add the dressing and toss gently to combine. Line a serving platter or individual plates with the salad greens, spoon the salad mixture on top, and serve.

45. Cranberry-Carrot Salad

- 1 pound carrots, shredded
- 1 cup sweetened dried cranberries
- 1/2 cup toasted walnut pieces
- 2 tablespoons fresh lemon juice
- 3 tablespoons toasted walnut oil
- 1/2 teaspoon sugar
- 1/4 teaspoon salt
- 1/8 teaspoon freshly ground black pepper

In a large bowl, combine the carrots, cranberries, and walnuts. Set aside.

In a small bowl, whisk together the lemon juice, walnut oil, sugar, salt, and pepper. Pour the dressing over the salad, toss gently to combine and serve.

46. Fennel-Orange Salad With Black Olives

- 1 medium fennel bulb, cut into 1/4-inch slices
- 2 oranges, peeled, quartered, and cut into 1/4-inch slices
- 1/4 cup kalamata olives, pitted and halved
- 2 tablespoons chopped fresh parsley
- 2 tablespoons olive oil
- 1 tablespoon lemon juice
- 1/2 teaspoon sugar
- Salt and freshly ground black pepper
- 4 large or 8 small Boston lettuce leaves
- 1/4 cup toasted pine nuts

In a large bowl, combine the fennel, oranges, olives, and parsley. Set aside.

In a small bowl, whisk together the oil, lemon juice, sugar, and salt and pepper to taste. Pour the dressing over the salad and toss gently to combine.

Arrange a layer of the lettuce leaves on a serving platter or individual plates. Spoon the salad on top of the lettuce, sprinkle with the pine nuts, and serve.

47. Yellow Beet Salad With Pears

- 3 to 4 medium yellow beets
- 2 tablespoons white balsamic vinegar
- 3 tablespoons vegan mayonnaise, homemade (see Vegan Mayonnaise) or store-bought
- 3 tablespoons vegan sour cream, homemade (see Tofu Sour Cream) or store-bought
- 1 tablespoon soy milk
- 11/2 tablespoons minced fresh dillweed
- 1 tablespoon minced shallot
- 1/2 teaspoon salt
- 1/8 teaspoon freshly ground black pepper
- 2 ripe Bosc pears
- Juice of 1 lemon
- 1 small head red leaf lettuce, torn into bite-size pieces

Steam the beets until tender, then cool and peel them. Cut the beets into matchsticks and place them in a shallow bowl. Add the vinegar and toss to coat. Set aside.

In a small bowl, combine the mayonnaise, sour cream, soy milk, dillweed, shallot, salt, and pepper. Set aside.

Core the pears and cut them into 1/4-inch dice. Place the pears in a medium bowl, add the lemon juice, and toss gently to combine. Divide the lettuce among 4 salad plates and spoon the pears and the beets on top. Drizzle the dressing over the salad, sprinkle with pecans, and serve.

48. Endive And Orange Salad

- 2 medium heads Belgian endive, leaves separated
- 2 navel oranges, peeled, halved, and cut into 1/4-inch slices
- 2 tablespoons minced red onion
- 3 tablespoons olive oil
- 11/2 tablespoons fig-infused balsamic vinegar
- Salt and freshly ground black pepper
- 1 tablespoon fresh pomegranate seeds (optional)

In a large bowl, combine the endive, oranges, pecans, and onion. Set aside.

In a small bowl, combine the oil, vinegar, sugar, and salt and pepper to taste. Stir until blended. Pour the dressing over the salad and toss gently to combine. Sprinkle with pomegranate seeds, if using, and serve.

CONCLUSION

Before getting into the specifics of the recipes and flavors in this book, it's important to plan the meal. You'll want to set the stage for your romantic dinner by making sure the two of you will be alone. If you have children, now's the time to call in that babysitting favor.

It's also a good idea to set some ground rules: Try agreeing to a no-tech evening, which might mean turning off the television or putting your phones out of sight. Scheduling might sound forced, but it's a great way to protect your relationship from the huge amount of 'life' constantly coming at you.

Once you've confirmed the date of your romantic evening, it's time to plan the menu. Be mindful of whether your fresh ingredients are in season, which can affect how easily you'll be able to source the necessary items on your list. Other things to consider include your dinner companion's dietary preferences and restrictions, like someone who prefers a plant-based diet or who has a nut allergy.

All that's left to do is turn on the tunes, enjoy your meal, and bask in each other's company—if you're enjoying each other, a romantic night at home beats a restaurant every time.

Lightning Source UK Ltd.
Milton Keynes UK
UKHW050843240521
384260UK00007B/56